JUNK FOOD

24 PAGE COLORING BOOK

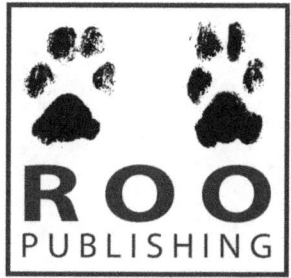

ROO
PUBLISHING

Illustrations by Dani Kates

Dear Colorer,

My name is Dani and I drew the pictures in this coloring book!
I'm an artist, a designer, and a HUGE fan of coloring.
When I buy a coloring book, the first thing I do is take a thin black pen and
draw tiny detailed lines and patterns to make the pictures more fun to color.
I love doing it so much that I decided to design my own coloring books with the
same type of detailed lines and fun patterns.

All of those details and lines make this is an "adult" style coloring book but the
pictures are way more fun to color!

This one is all about Junk Food!
Hamburgers, hot dogs, milkshakes...and so much more!

So have fun, color something amazing and share it with me on social media!

@DaniKatesColoringBooks
#DaniKatesColoringBooks

XOXO,
Dani Kates

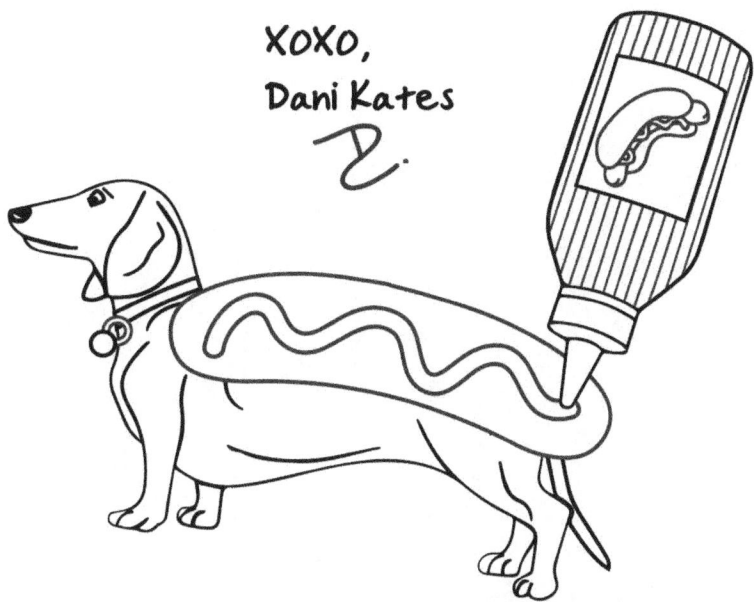

P.S. This is my favorite drawing from this book!
also, a big thank you to Stephanie Kole for her ideas!

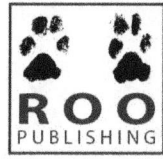

ROO
PUBLISHING

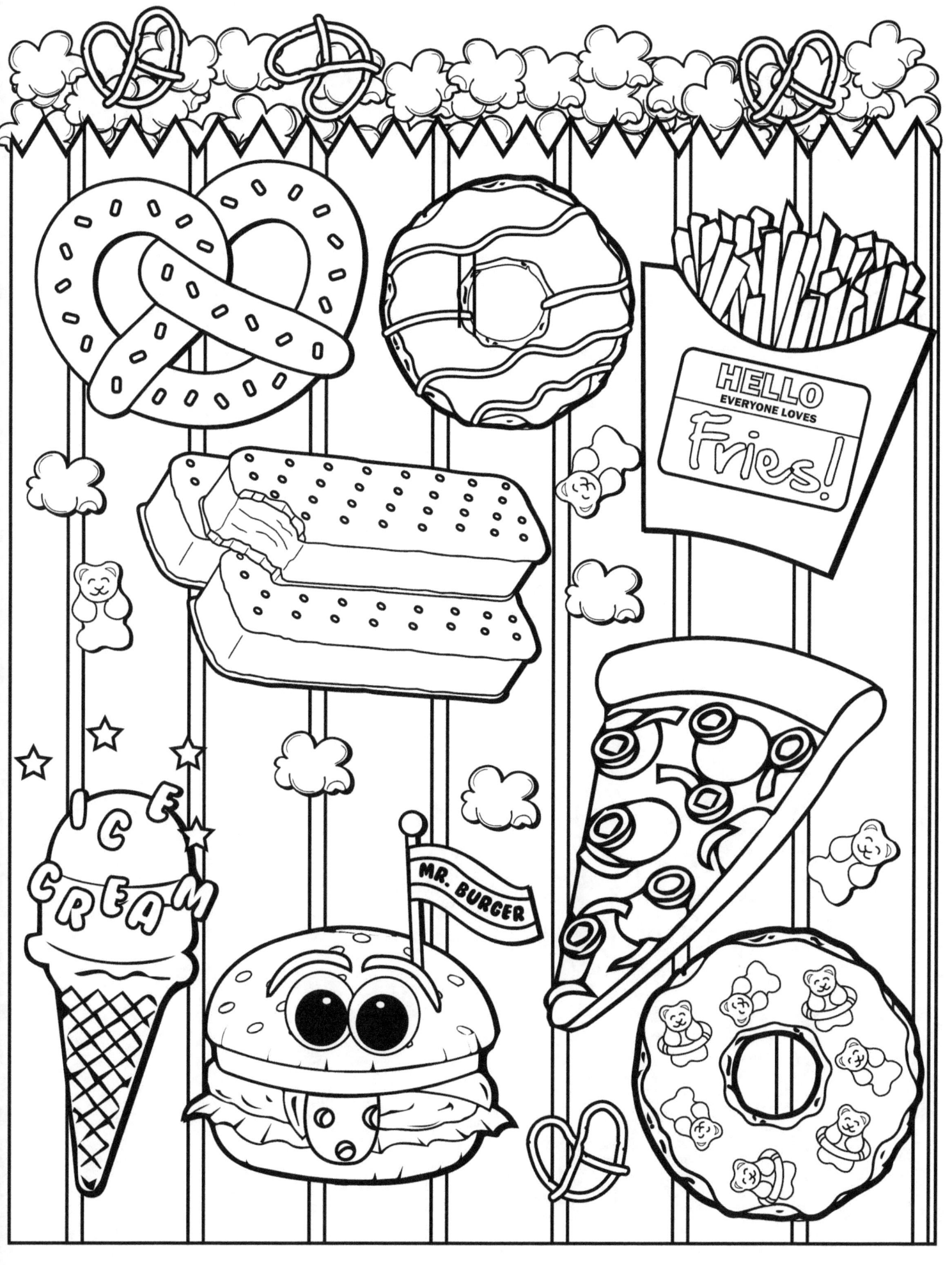

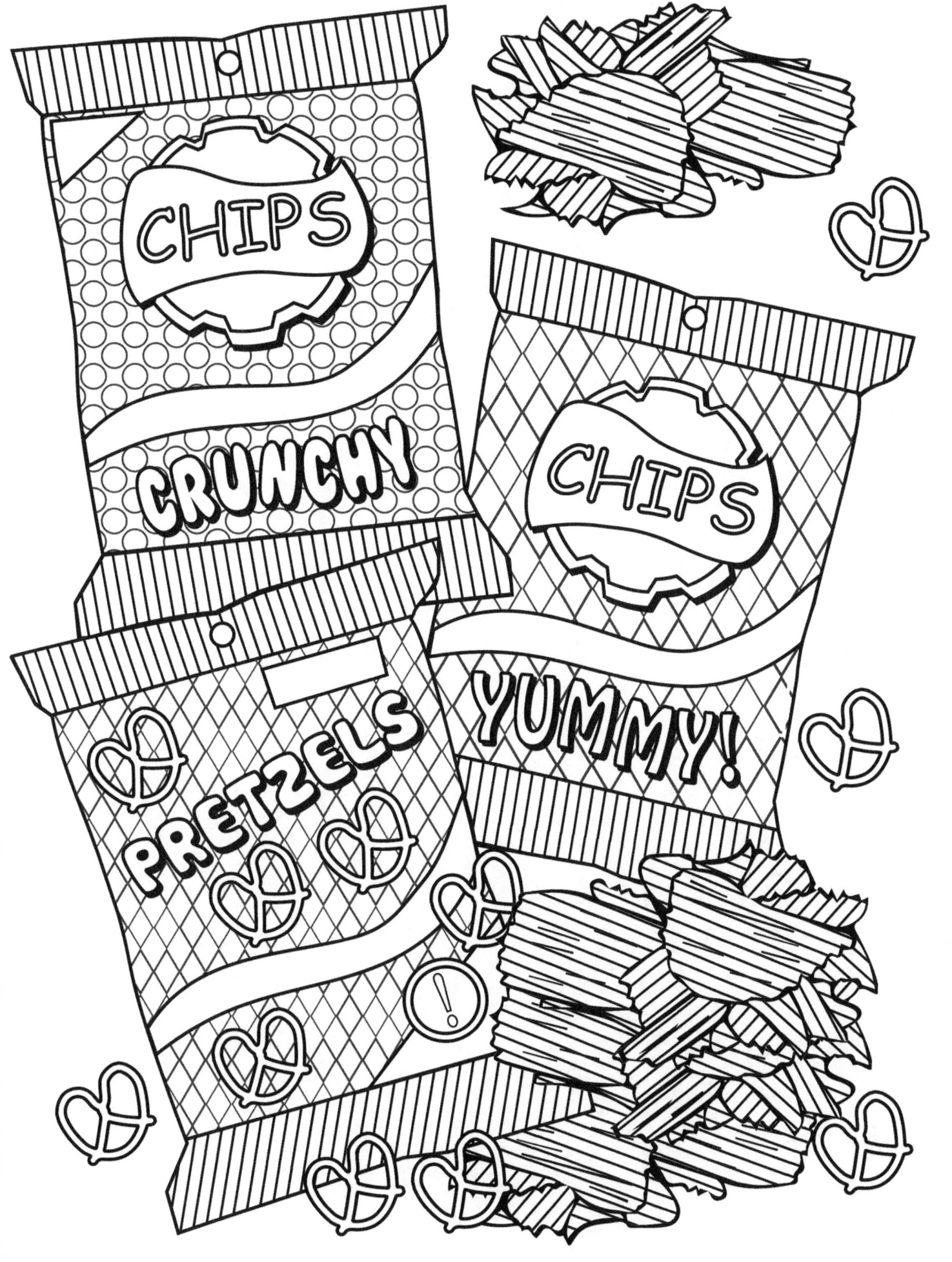

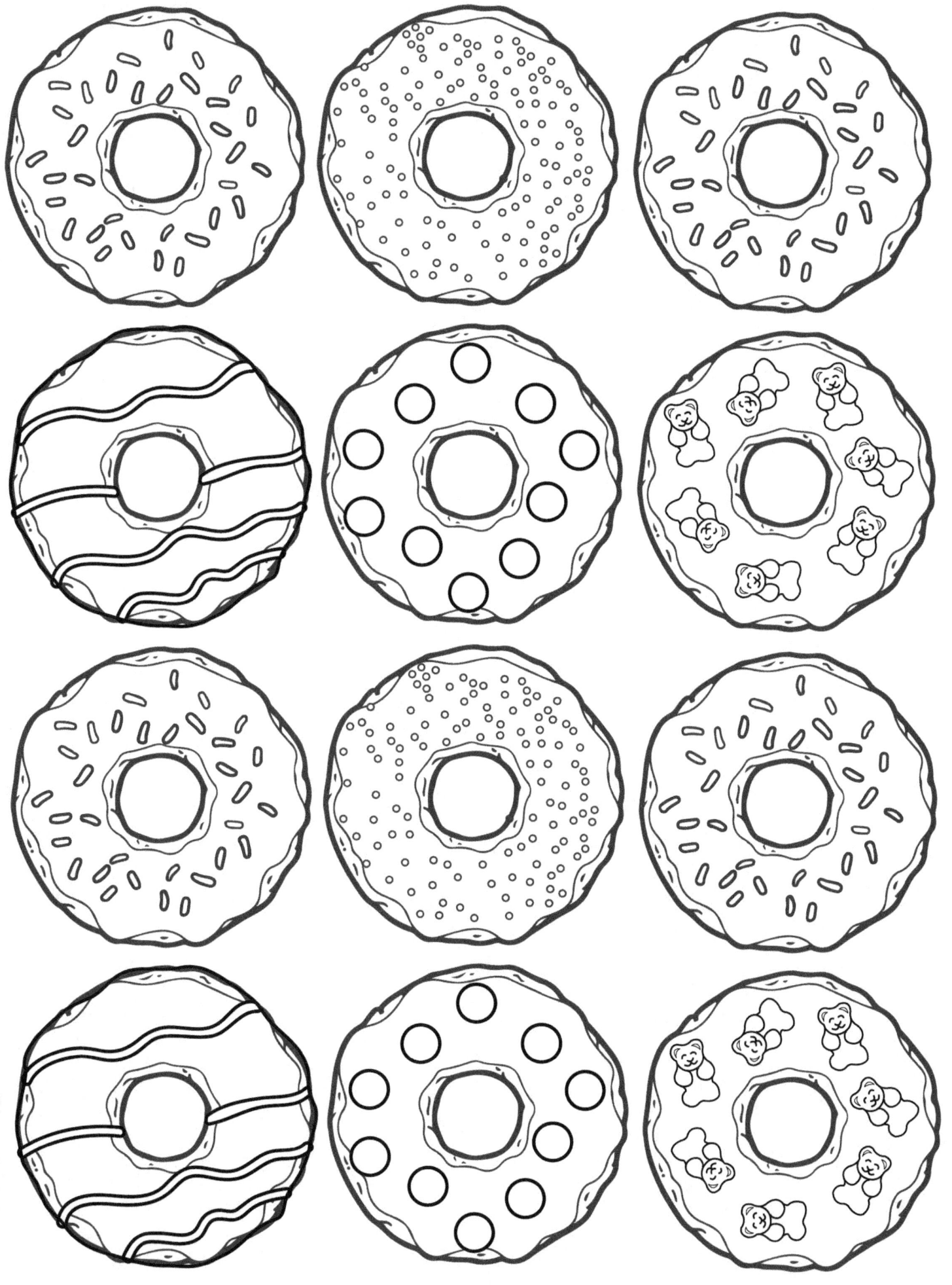

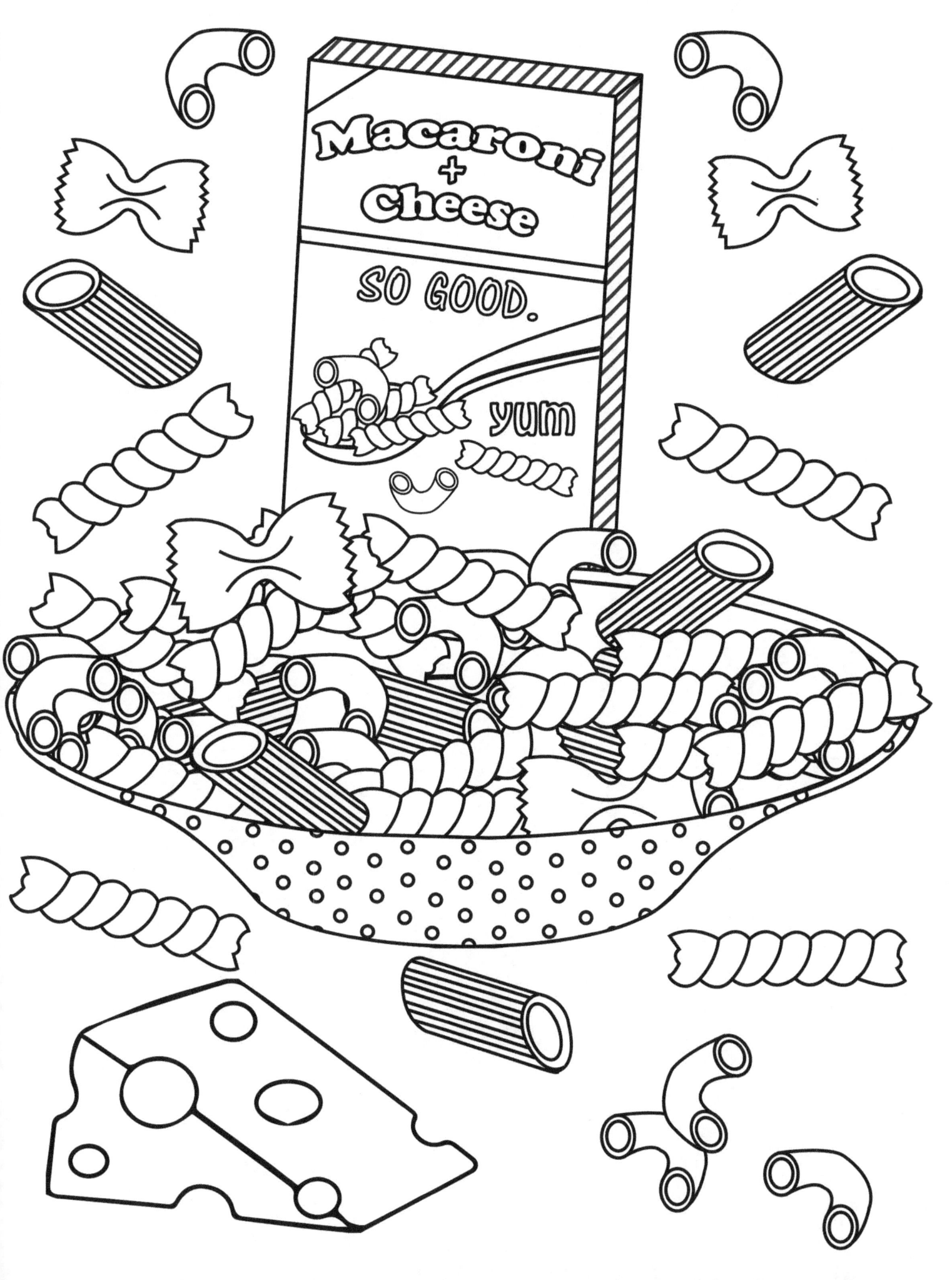

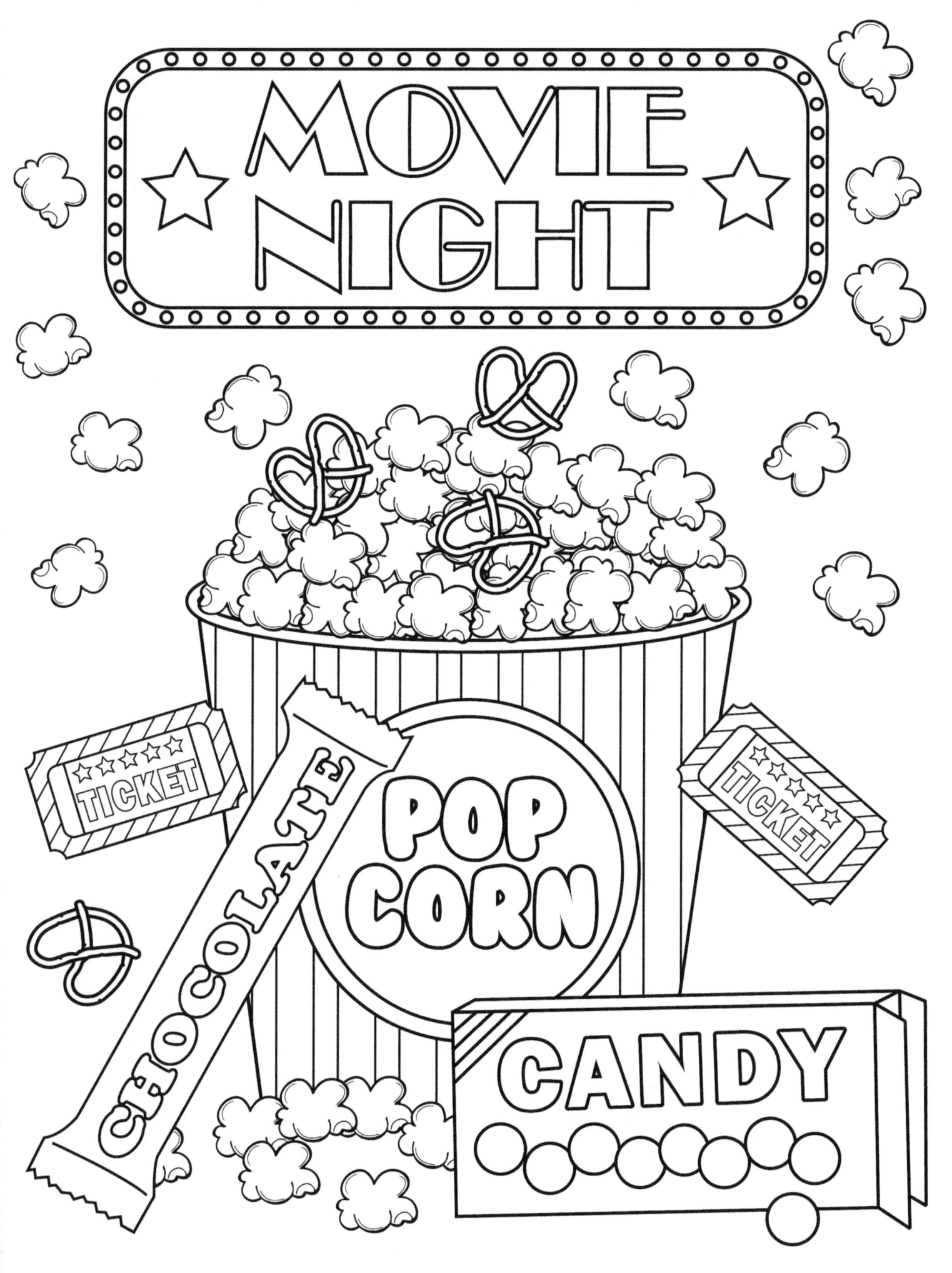

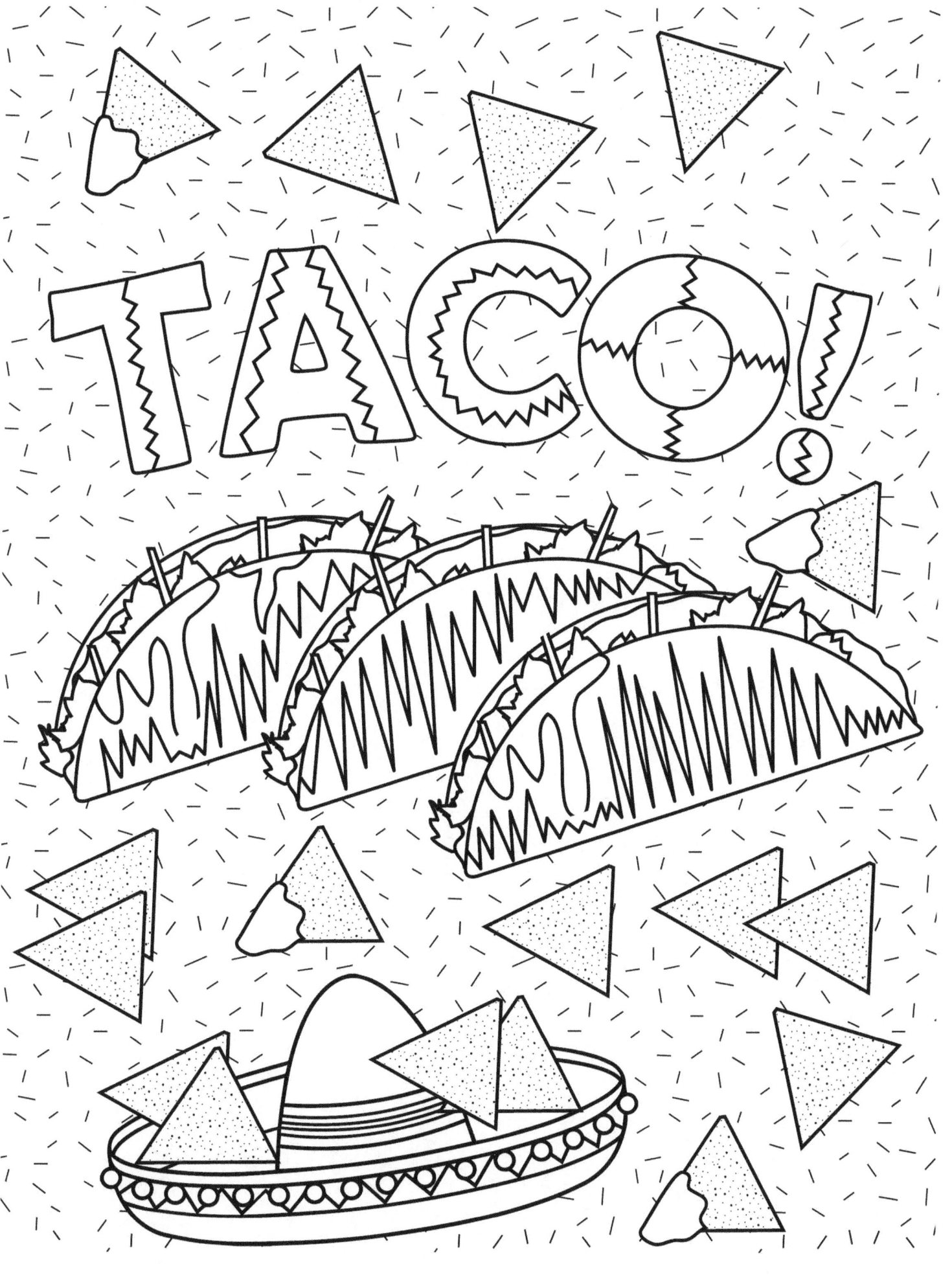

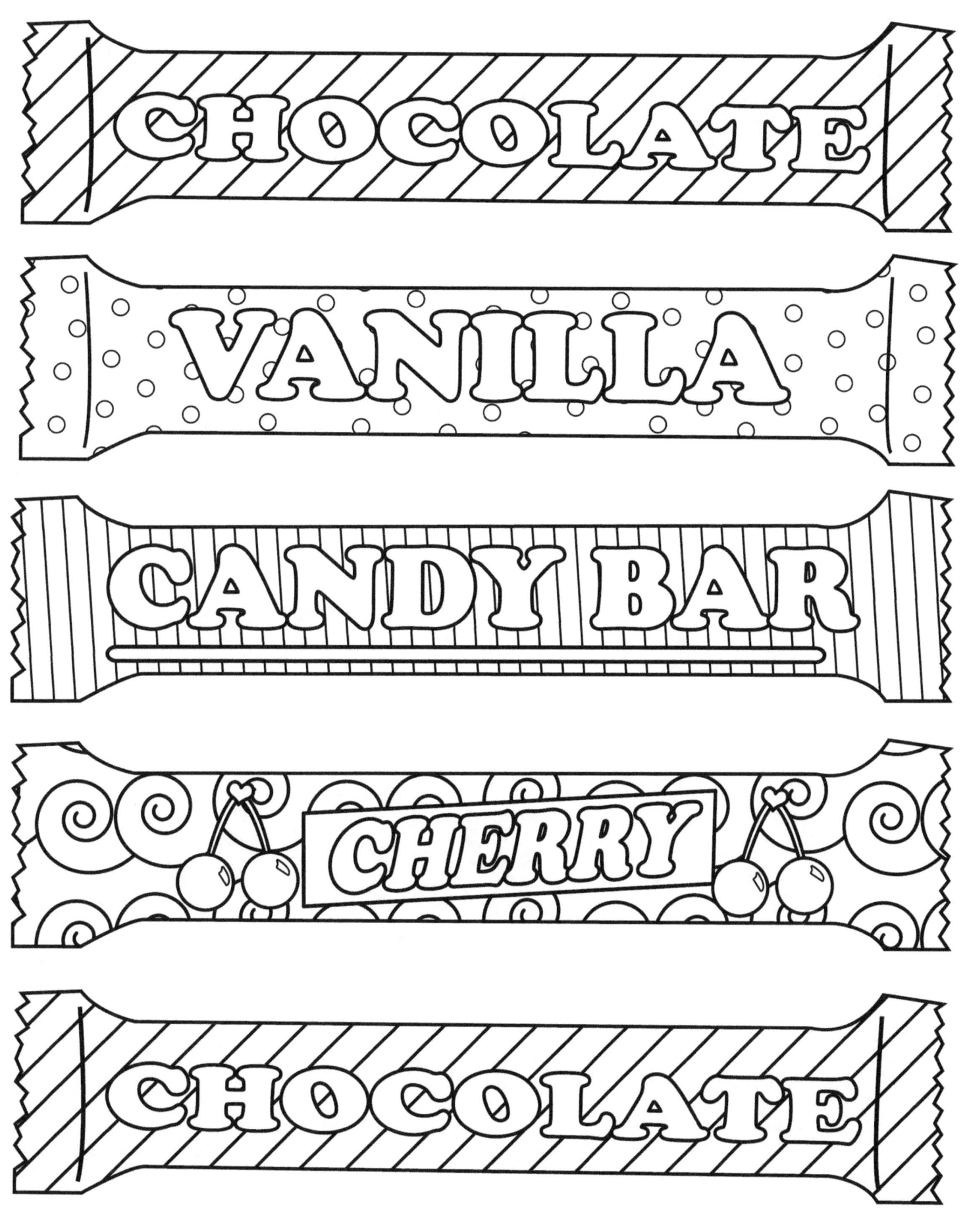

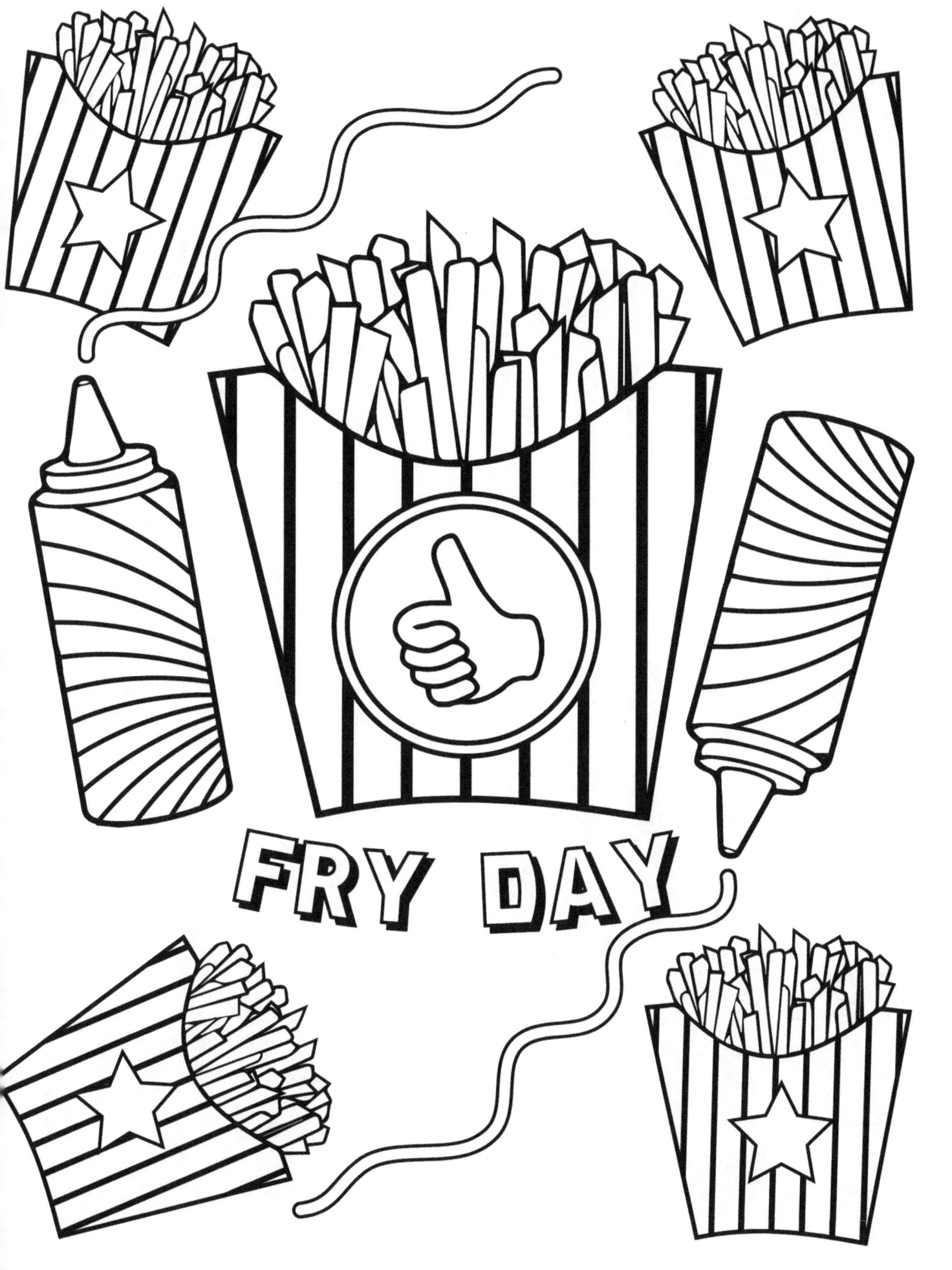

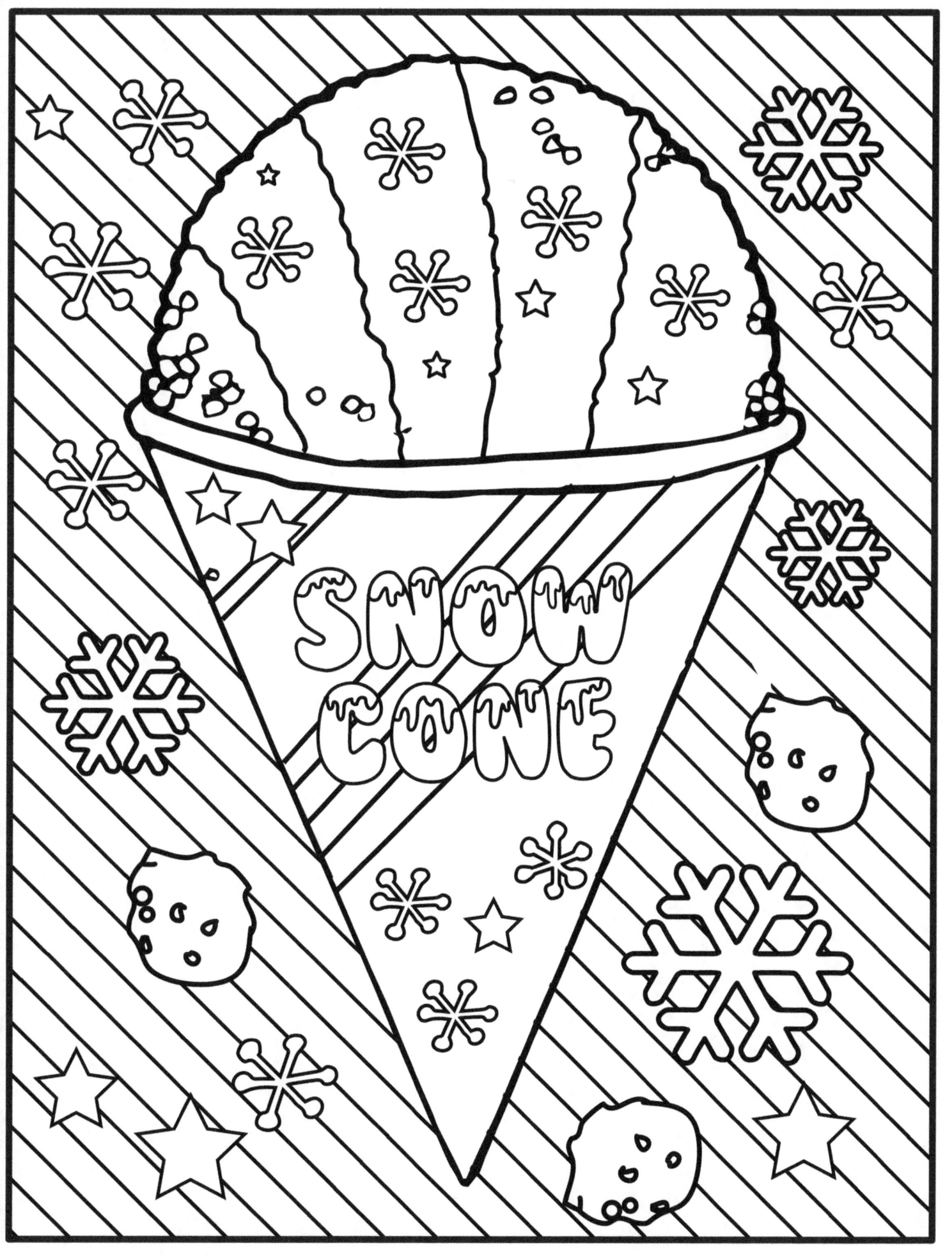

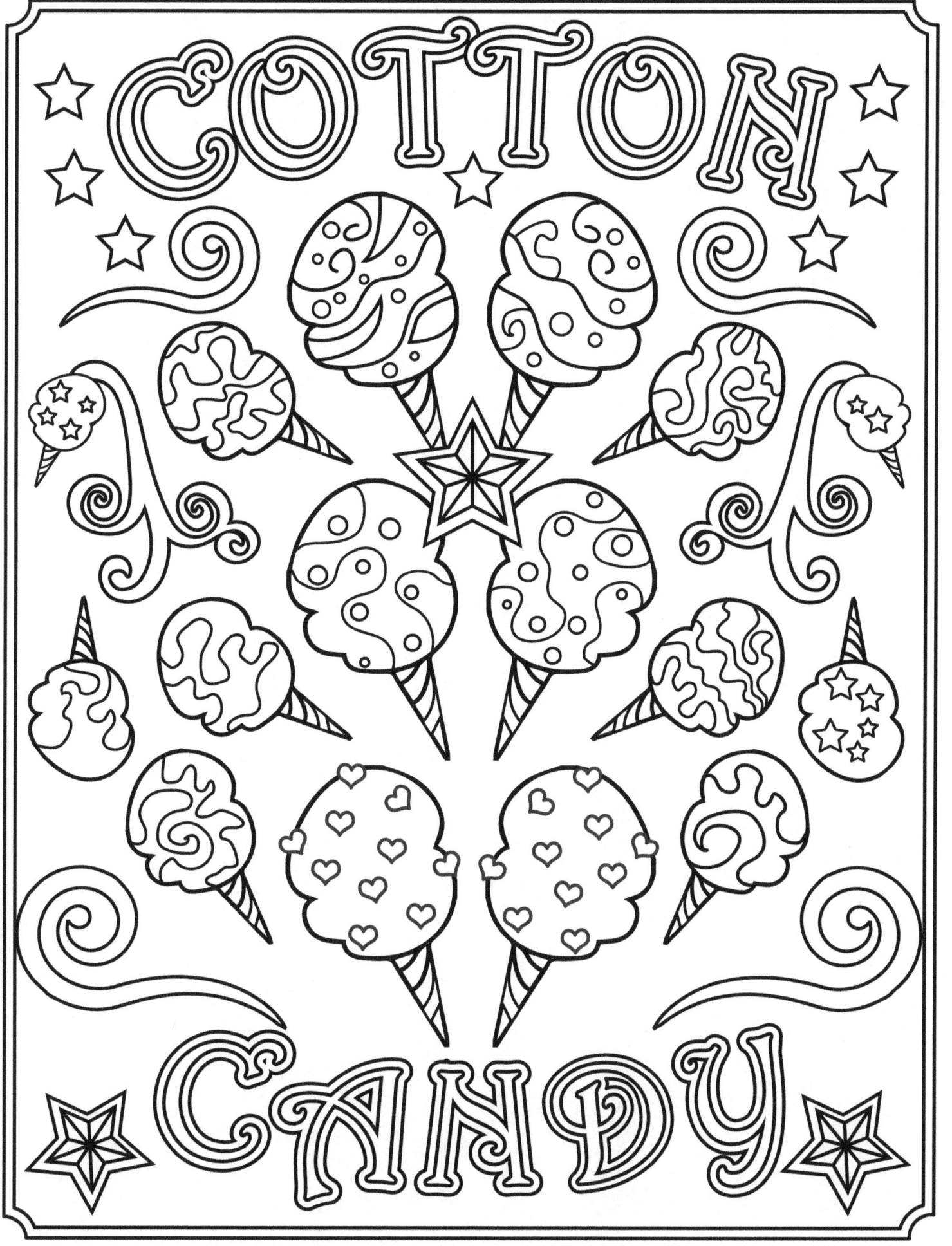

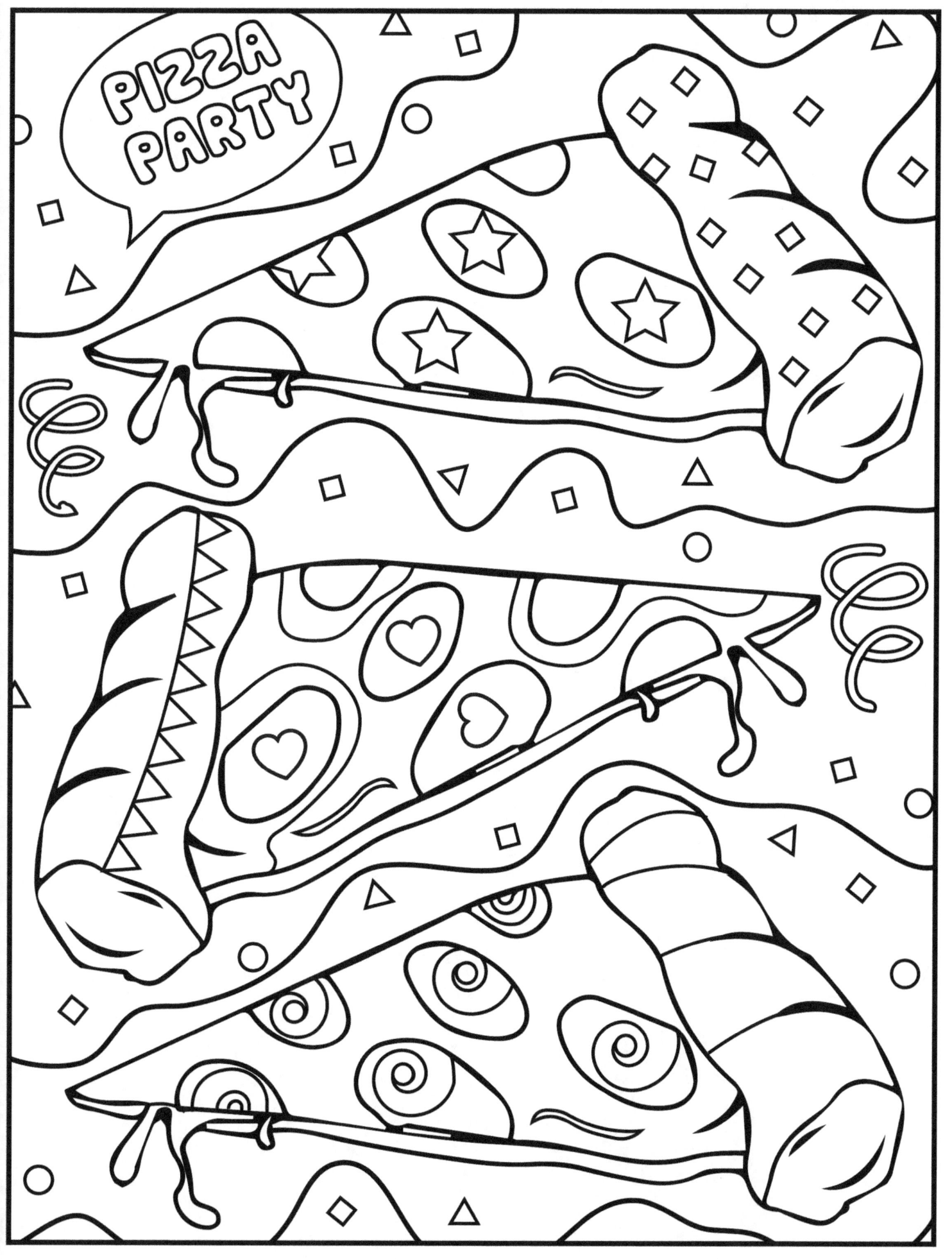

PIZZA
DONUTS
COOKIES
ice cream
CANDY
POPCORN

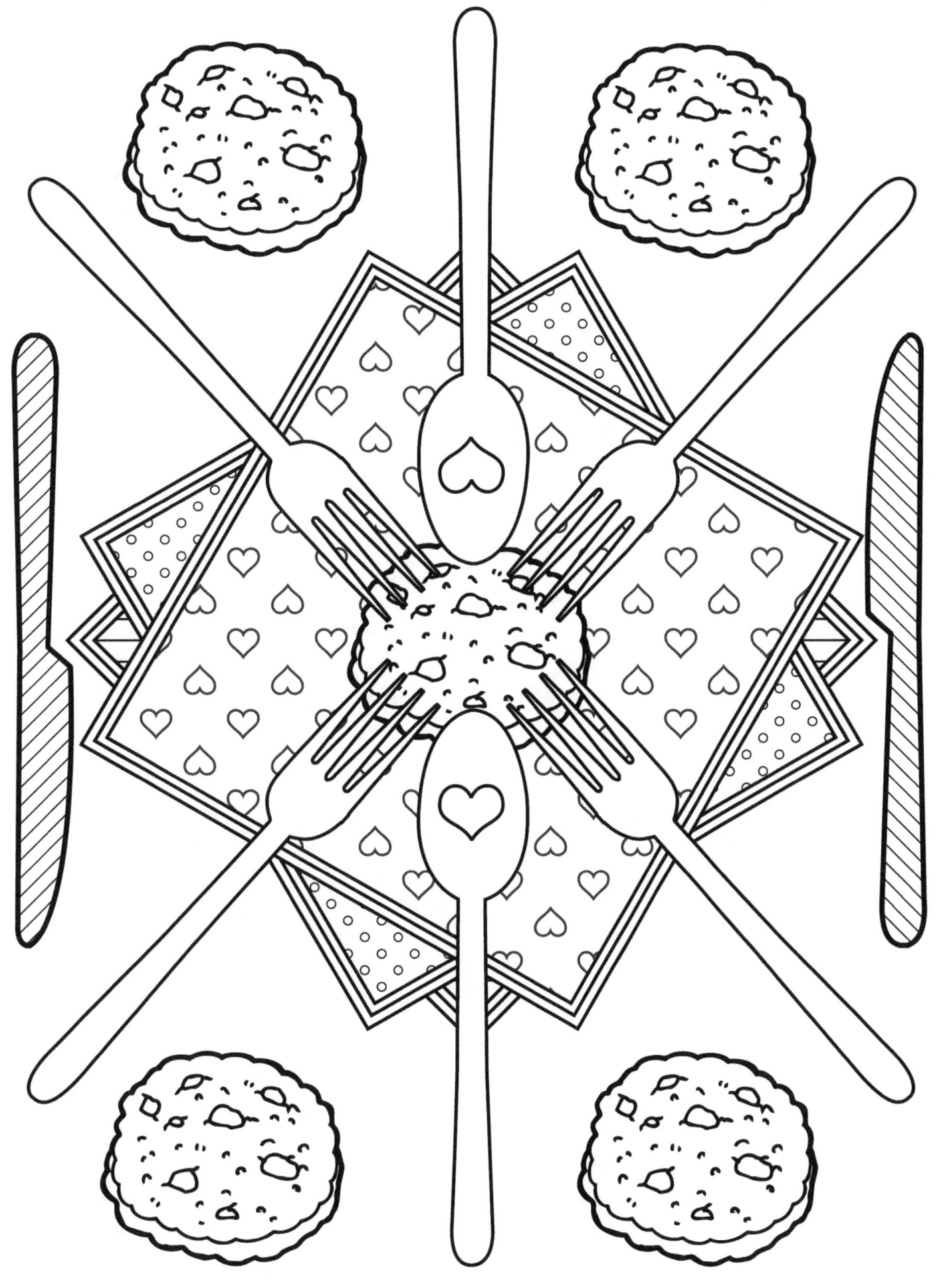

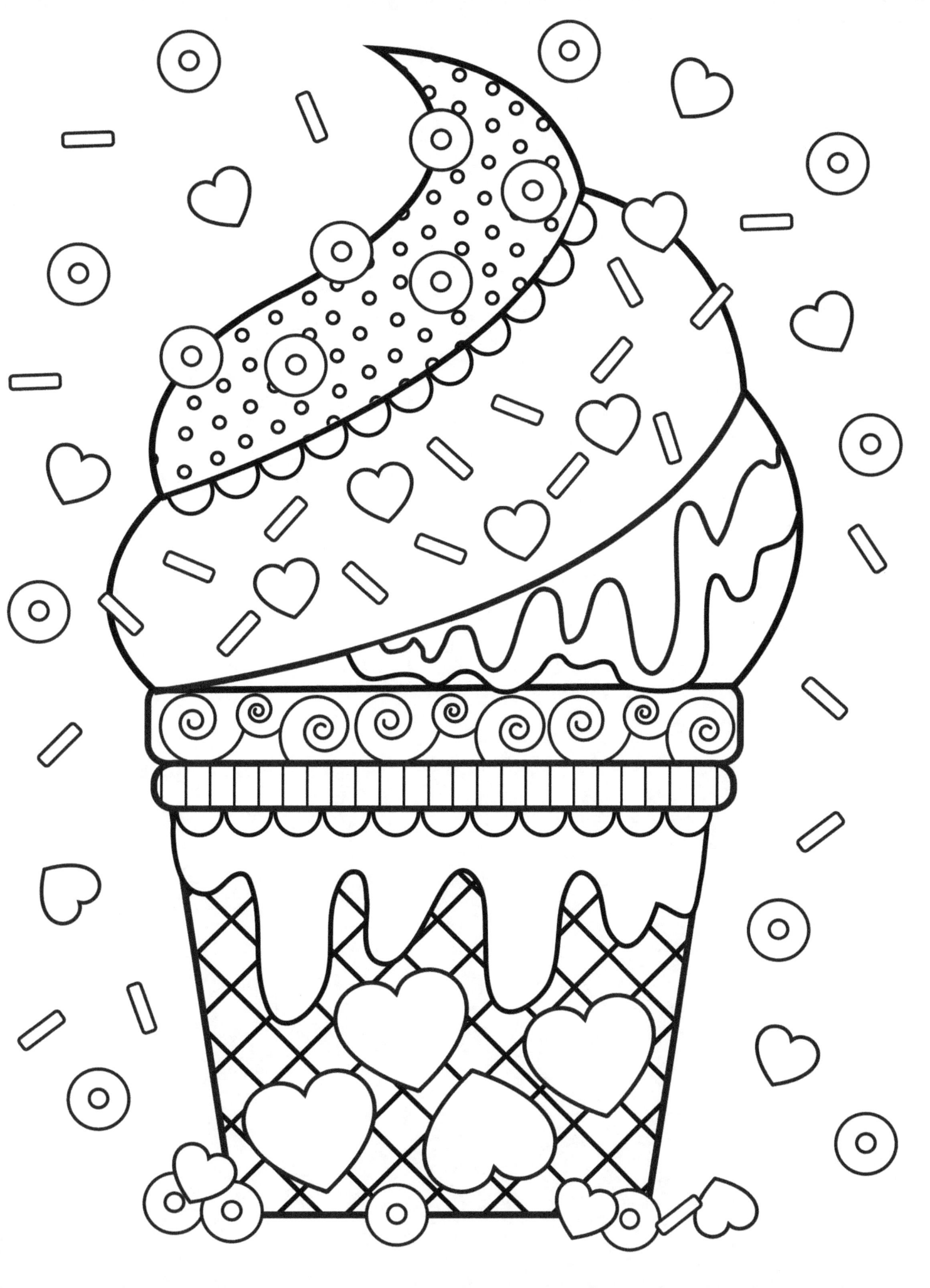

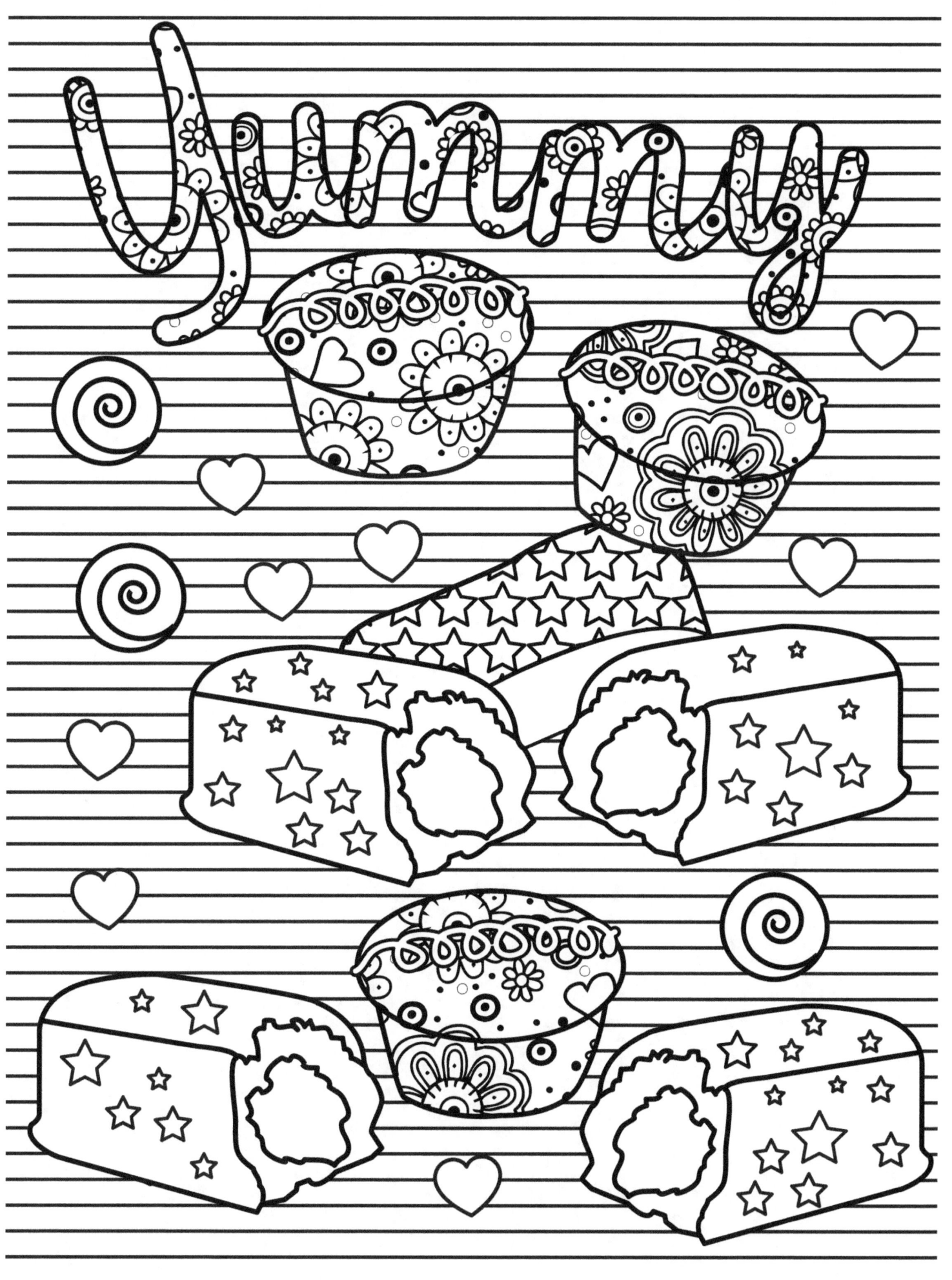

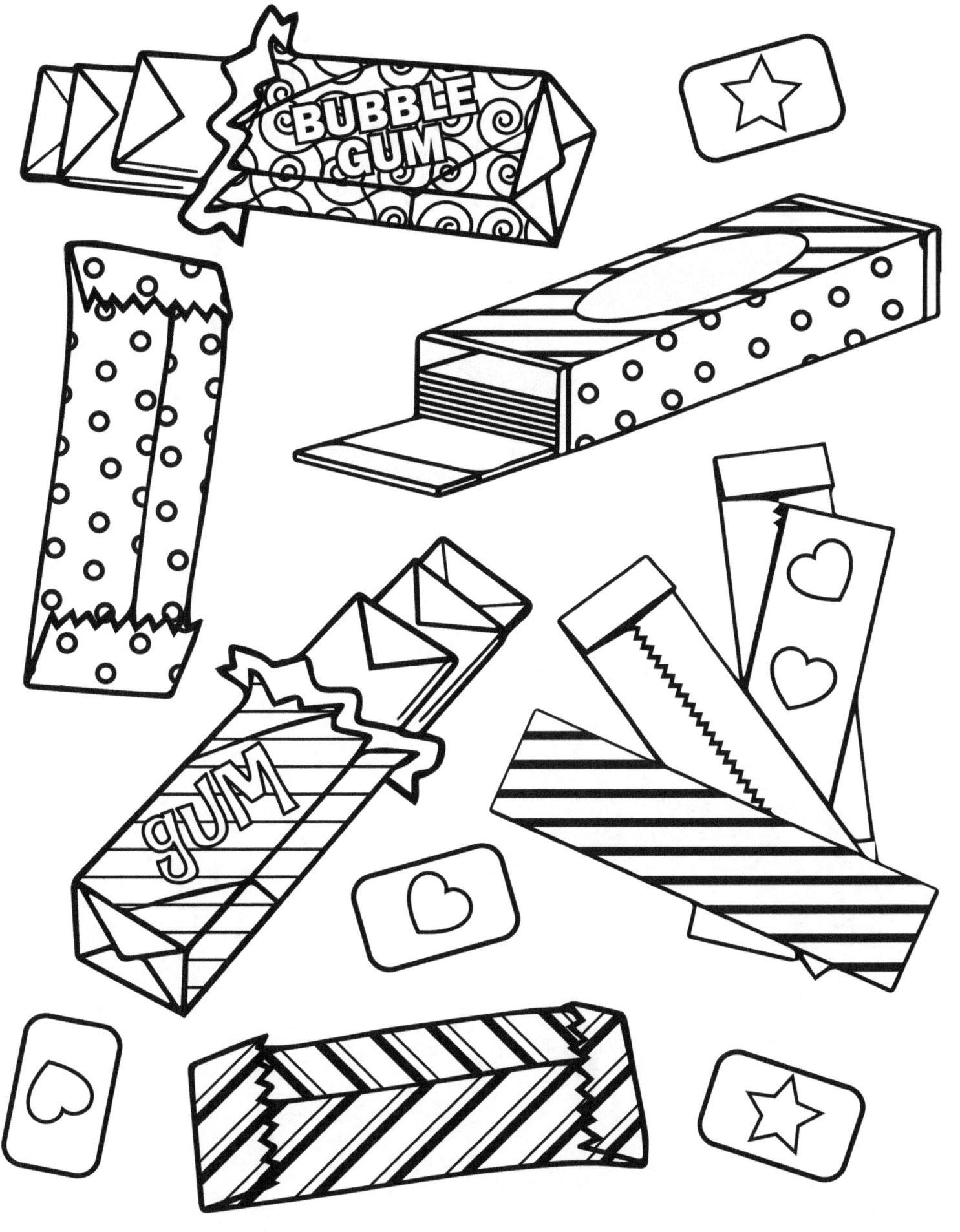

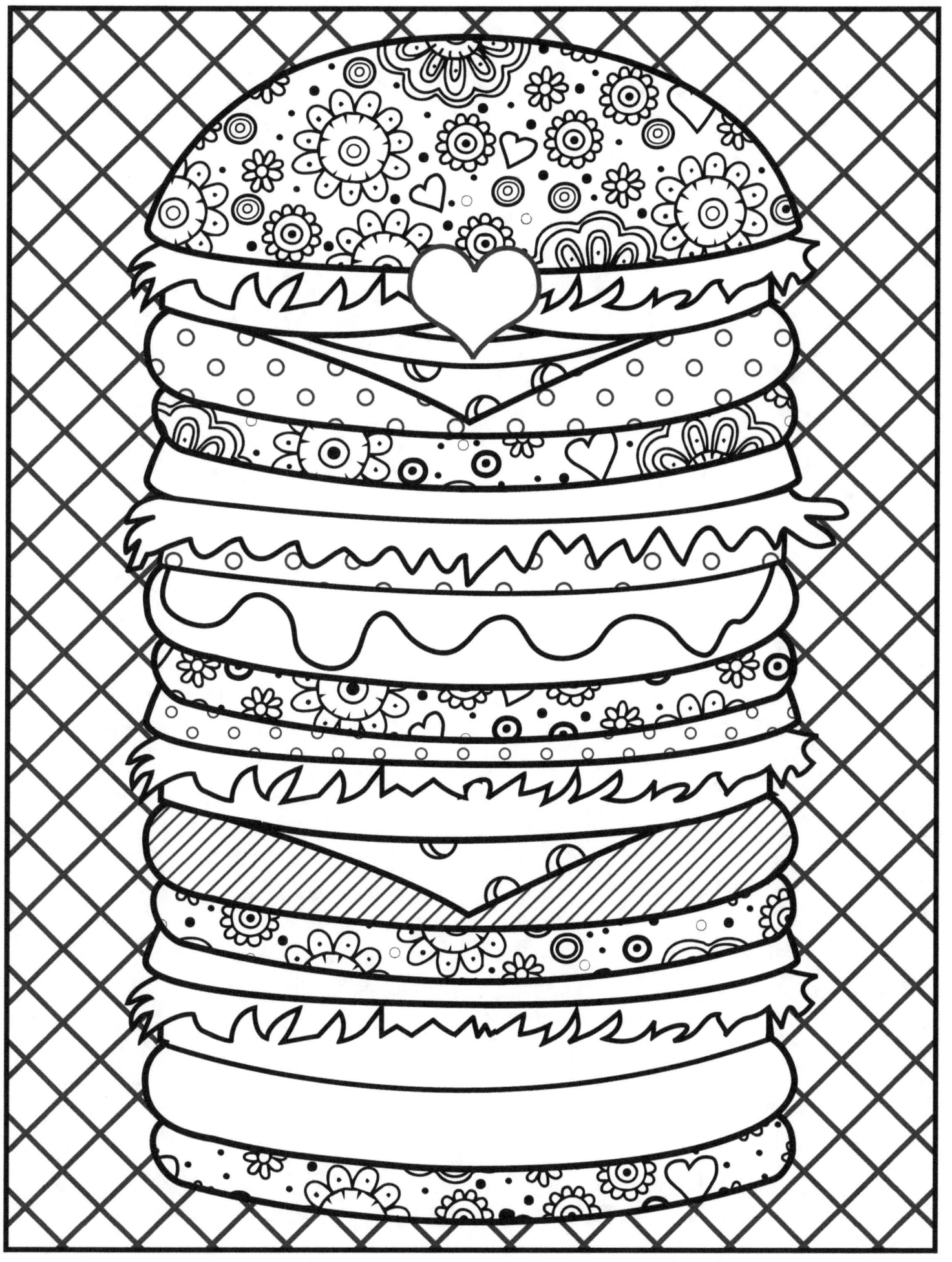

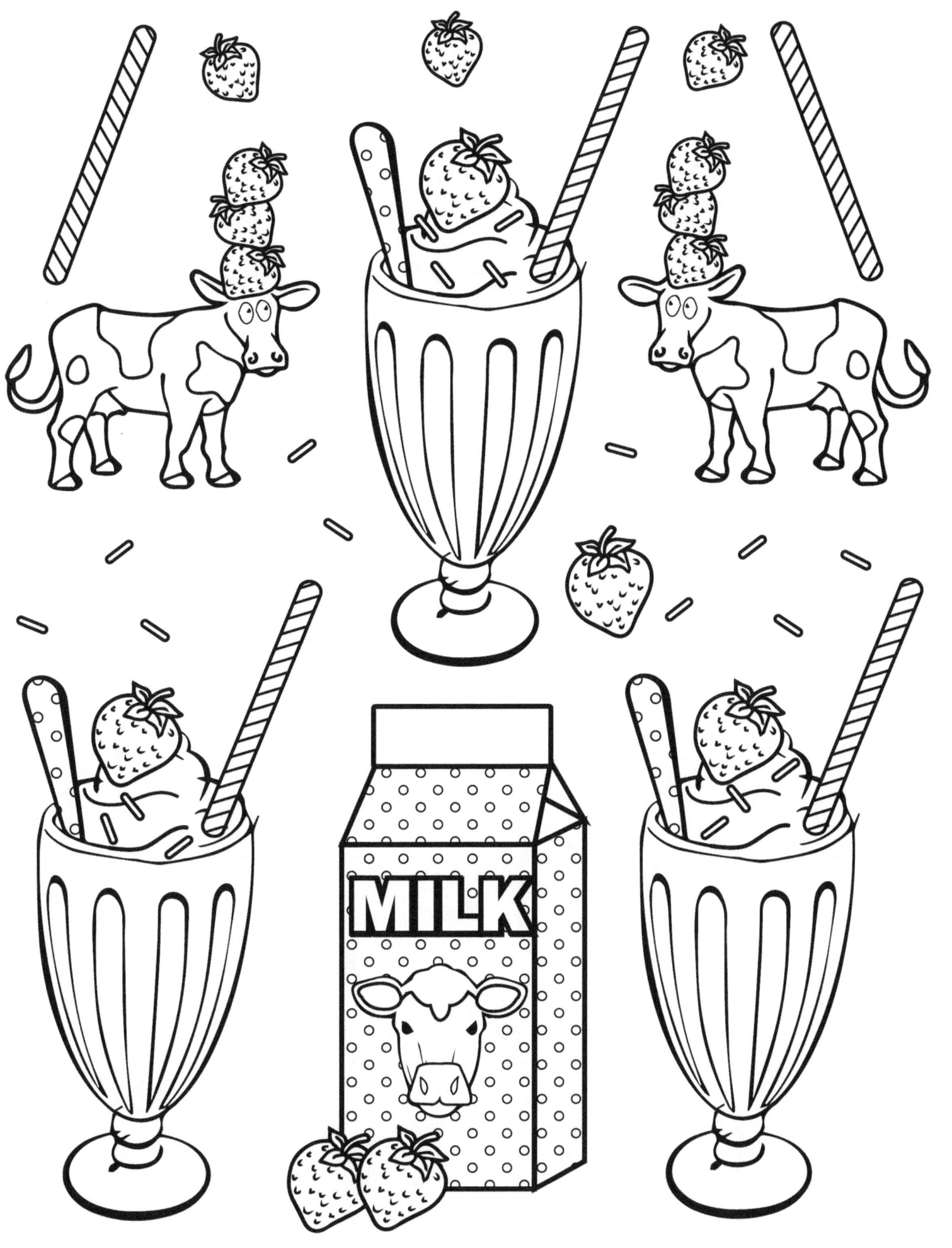

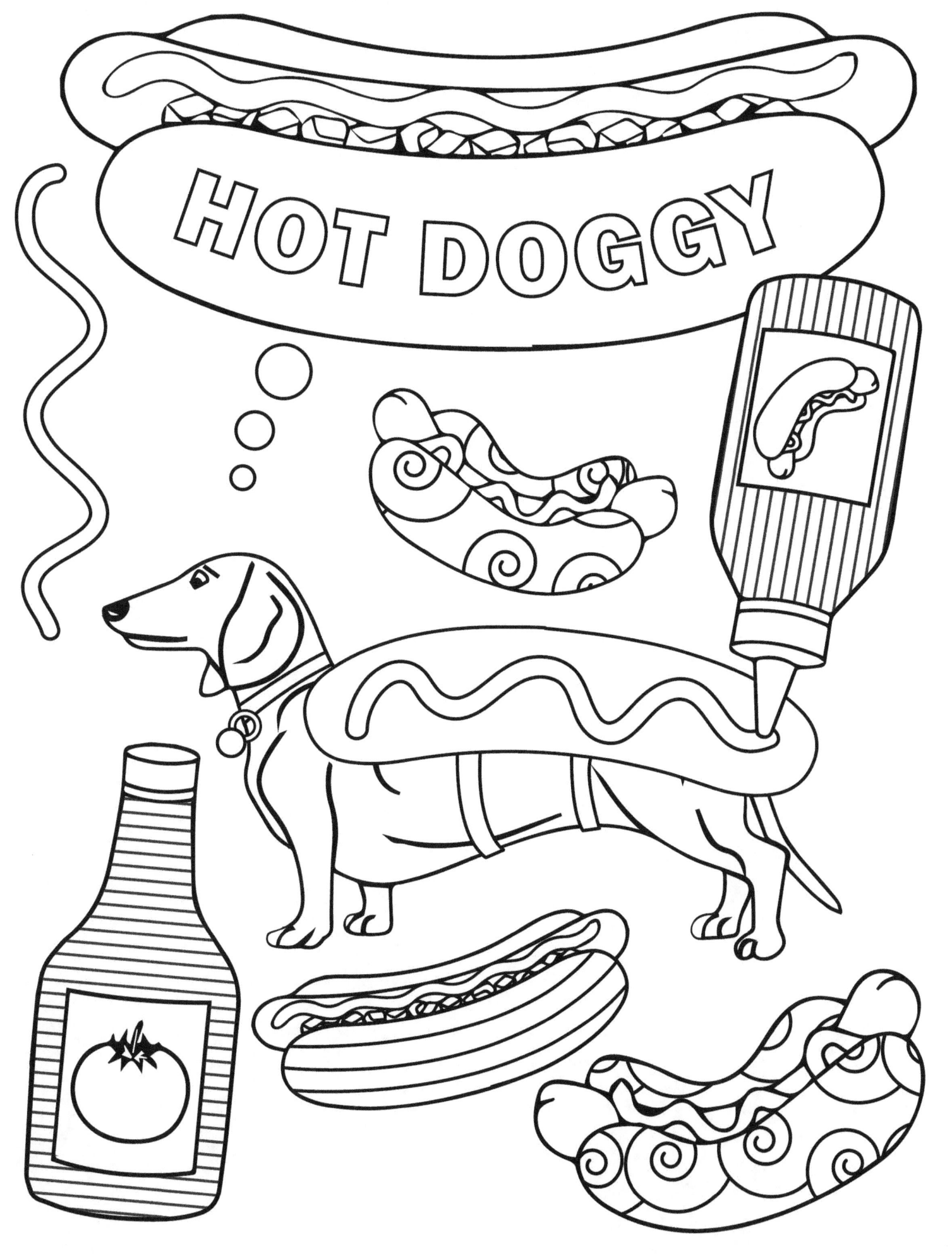

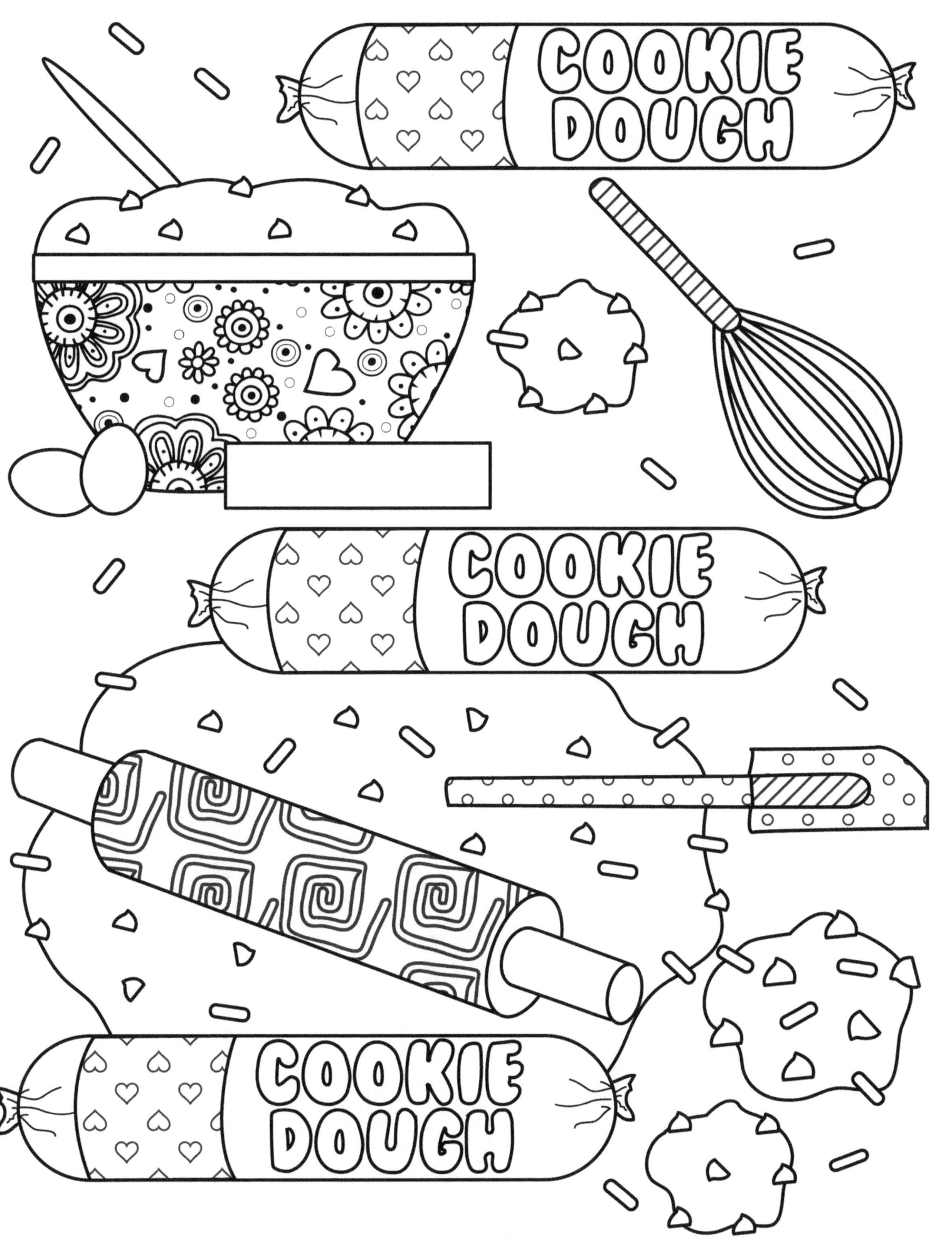

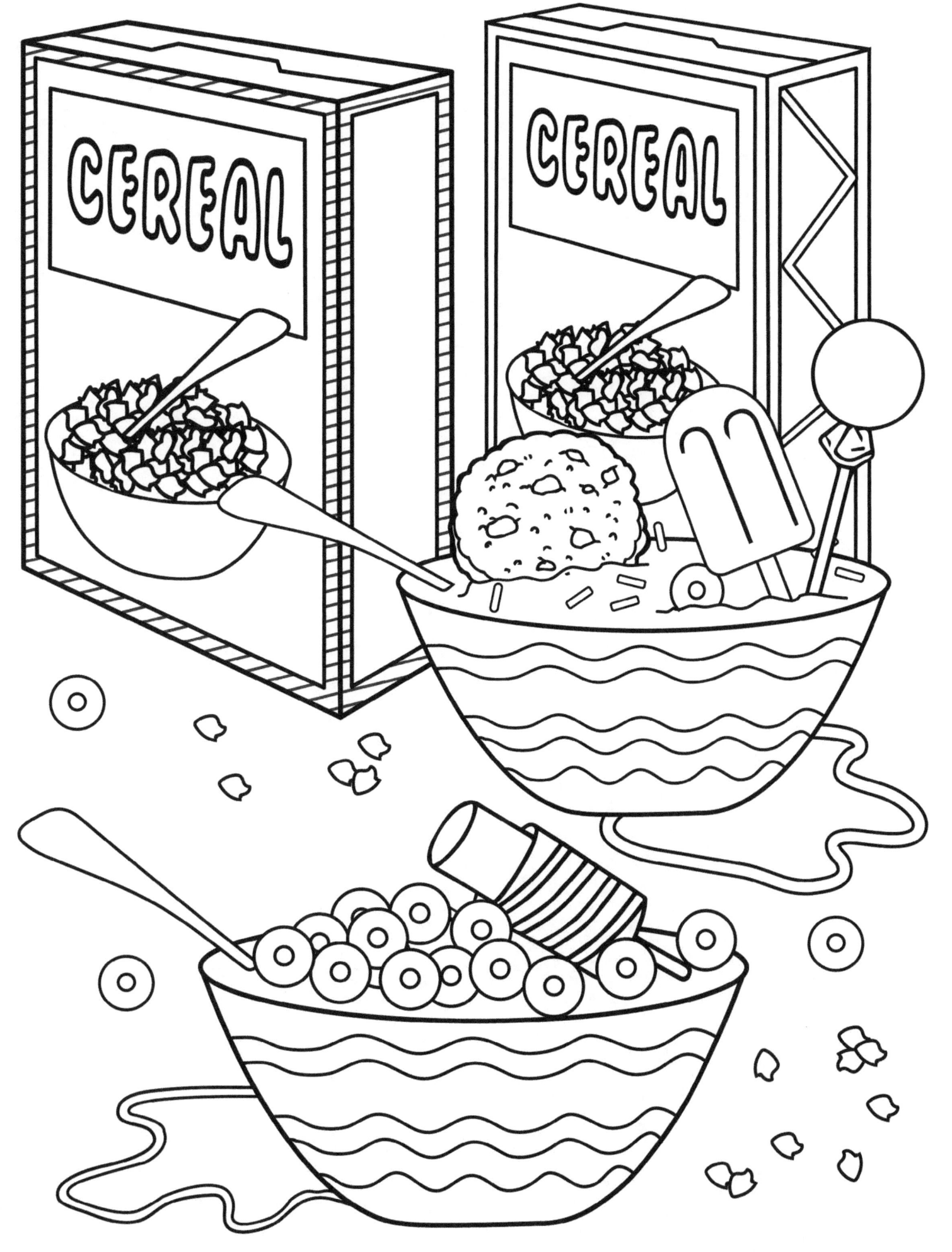

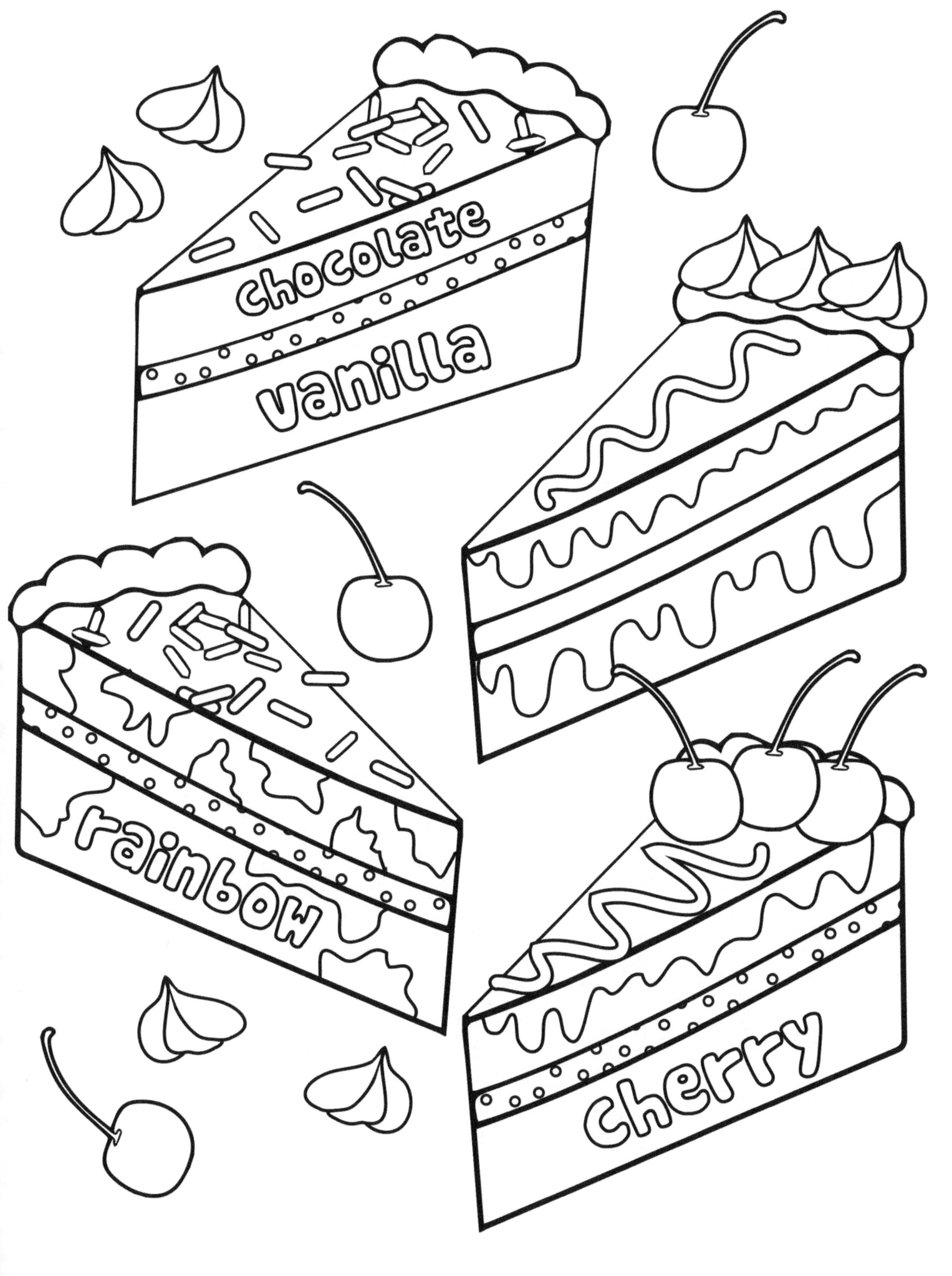

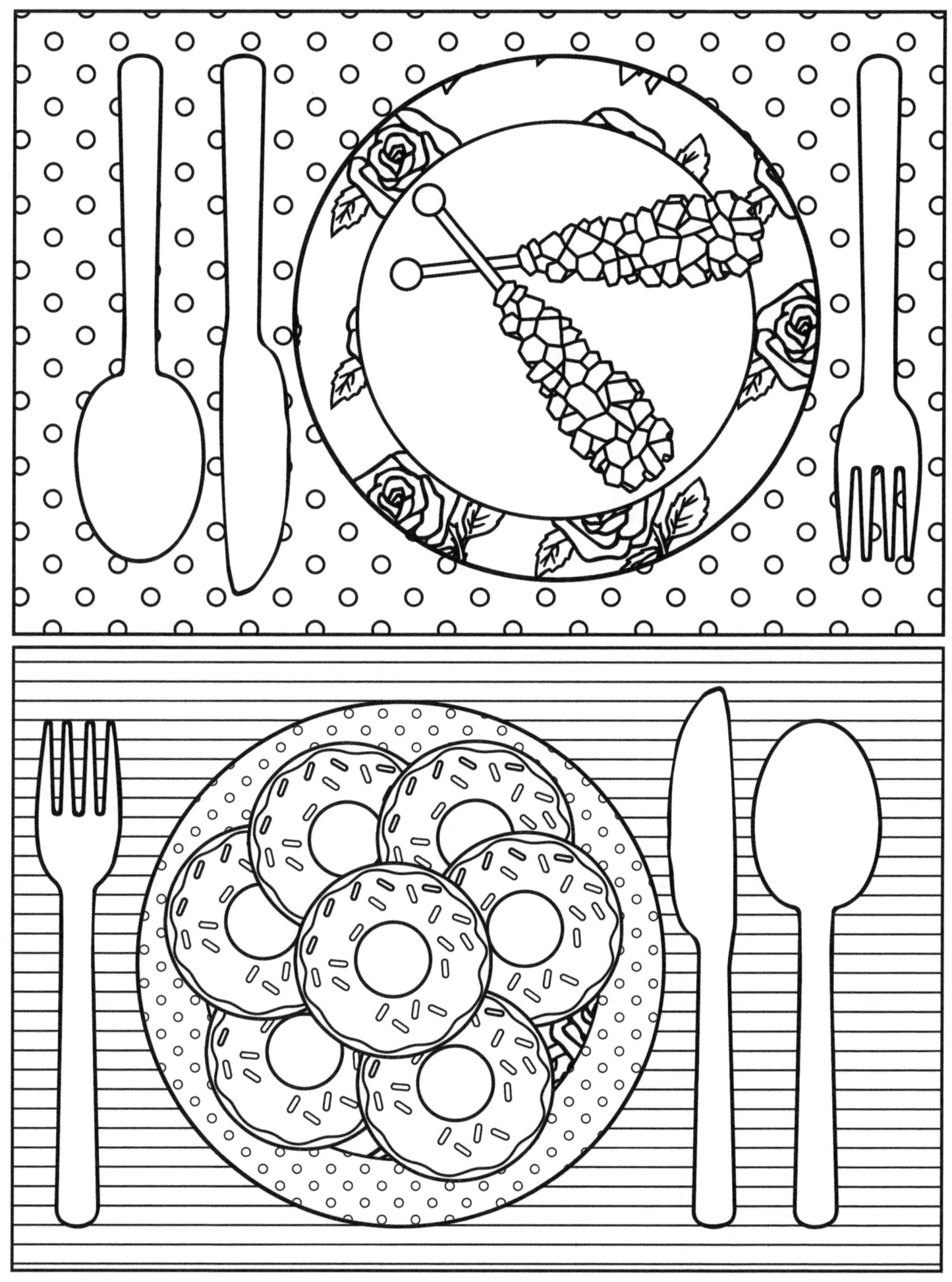

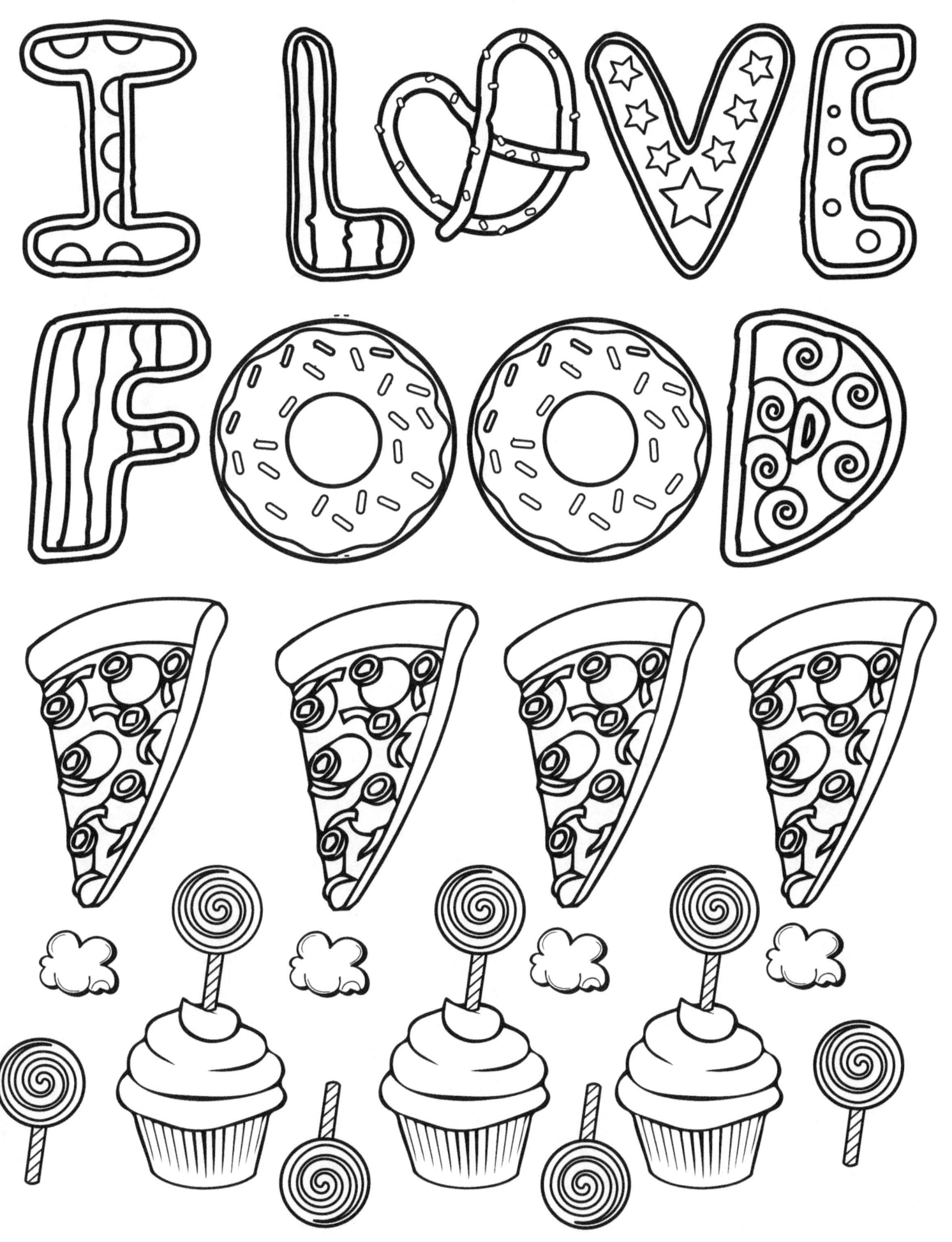

www.ingramcontent.com/pod-product-compliance
Lightning Source LLC
Chambersburg PA
CBHW080603190526
45169CB00007B/2862